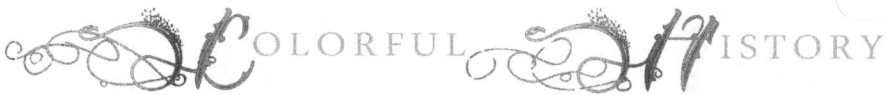

Colorful History

# LEGENDS

## VOLUME I

ORIGINAL ART BY KASI HEWETT . ORIGINAL TEXTS BY SEAMUS KING

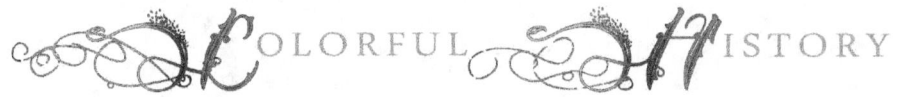

COLORFULHISTORY.WORDPRESS.COM

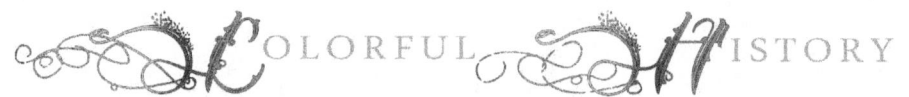

THIS VOLUME IS PUBLISHED UNDER THE REIGN OF AND DEDICATED TO

THEIR ROYAL MAJESTIES WULFSTAN AND THORKATLA.

ALSO TO THEIR ROYAL HIGHNESSES ADHEMAR AND ELINA,

THE SHIRE OF FORTH CASTLE, THE BARONY OF THOR'S MOUNTAIN,

AND THE KINGDOM OF MERIDIES.

CORONA VULT!

A.S. 50

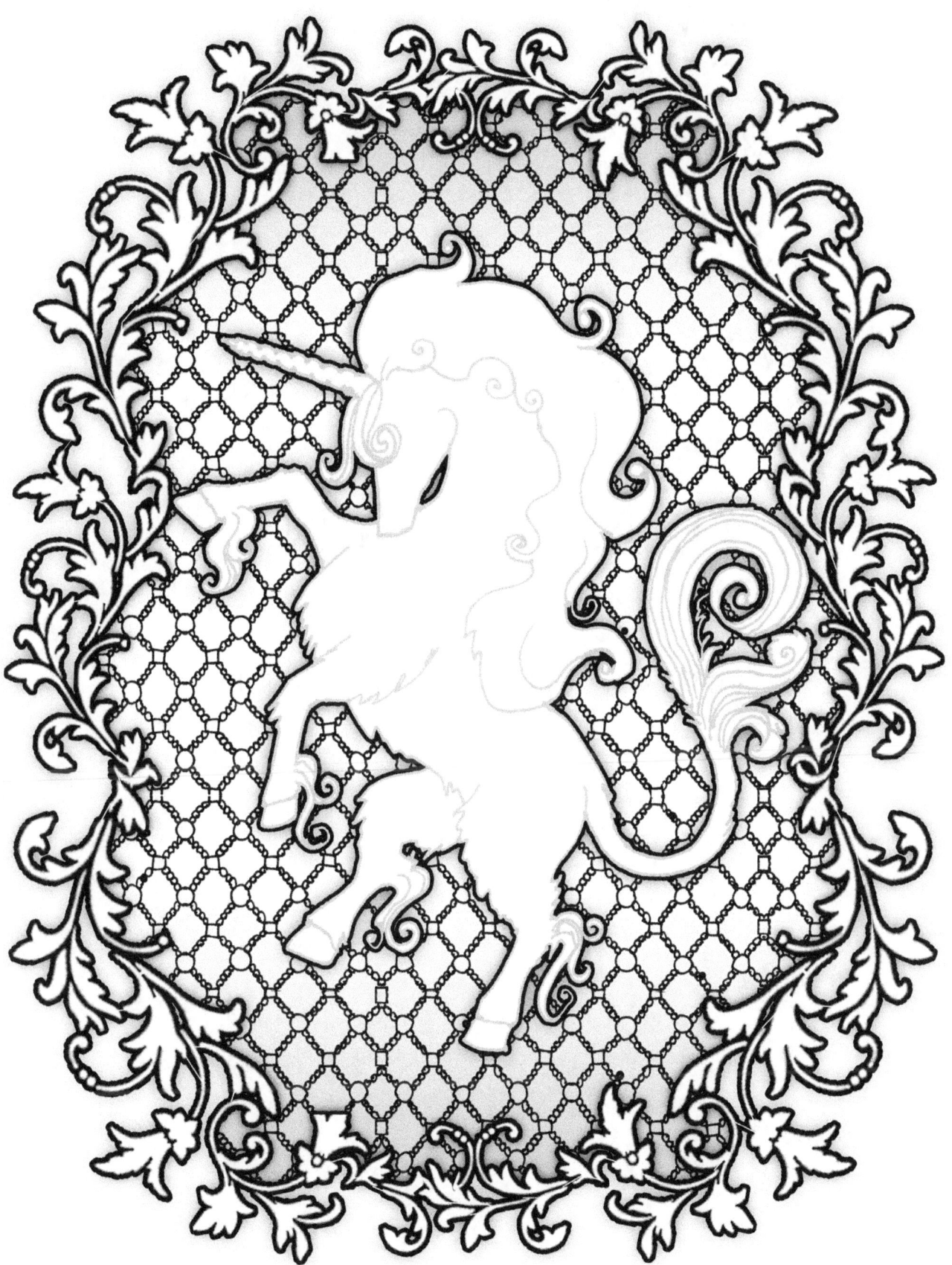

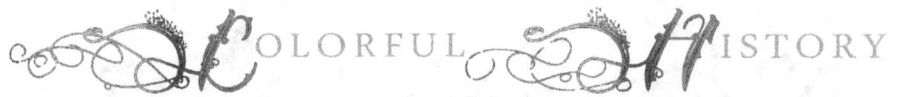
### THE
# UNICORN

COURAGE . VIRTUE . STRENGTH

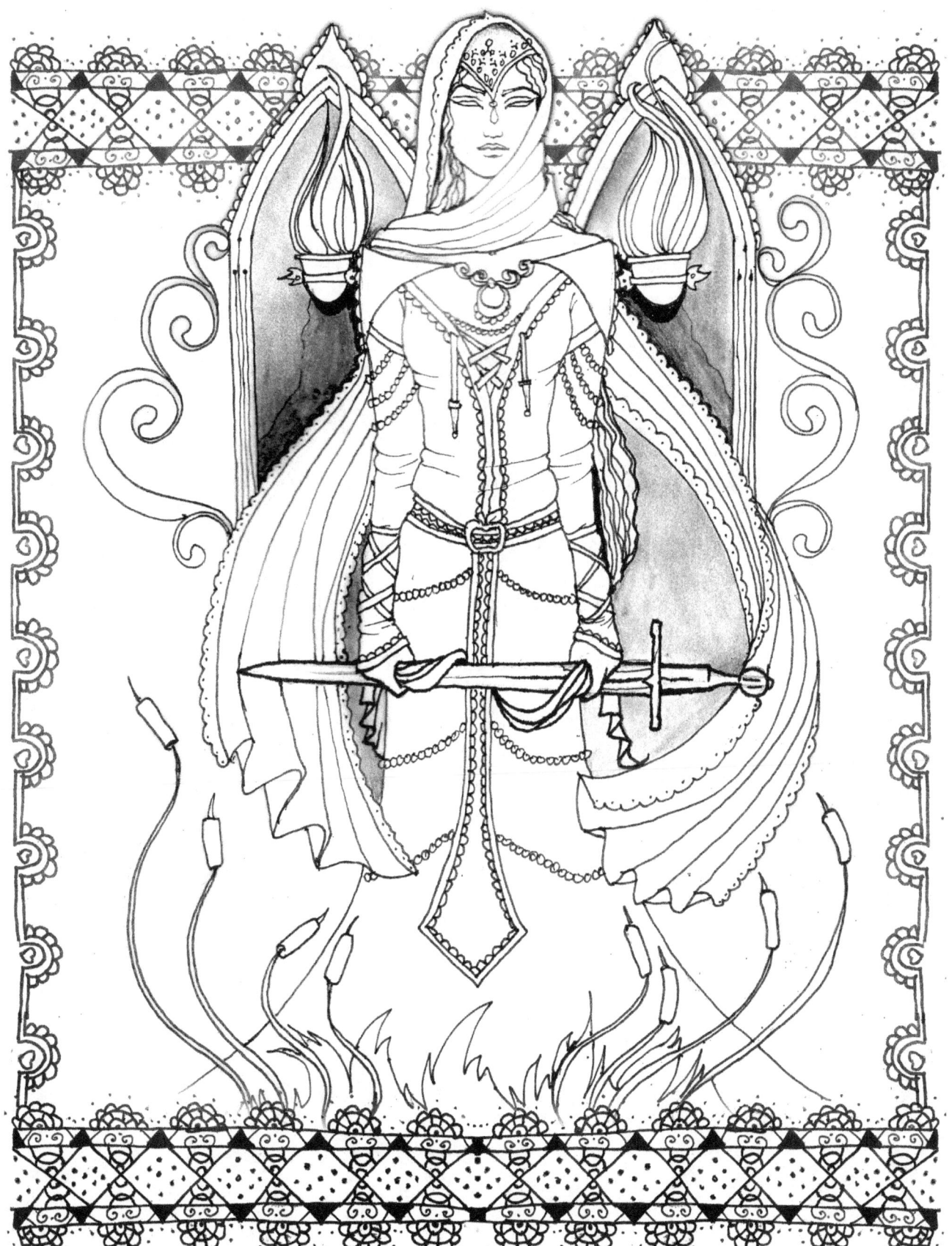

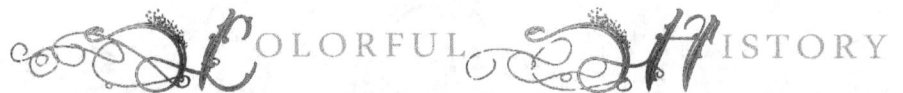

AND NEAR HIM STOOD THE LADY OF THE LAKE,

WHO KNOWS A SUBTLER MAGIC THAN HIS OWN —

CLOTHED IN WHITE SAMITE, MYSTIC, WONDERFUL.

SHE GAVE THE KING HIS HUGE CROSS-HILTED SWORD,

WHEREBY TO DRIVE THE HEATHEN OUT

(ALFRED, LORD TENNYSON)

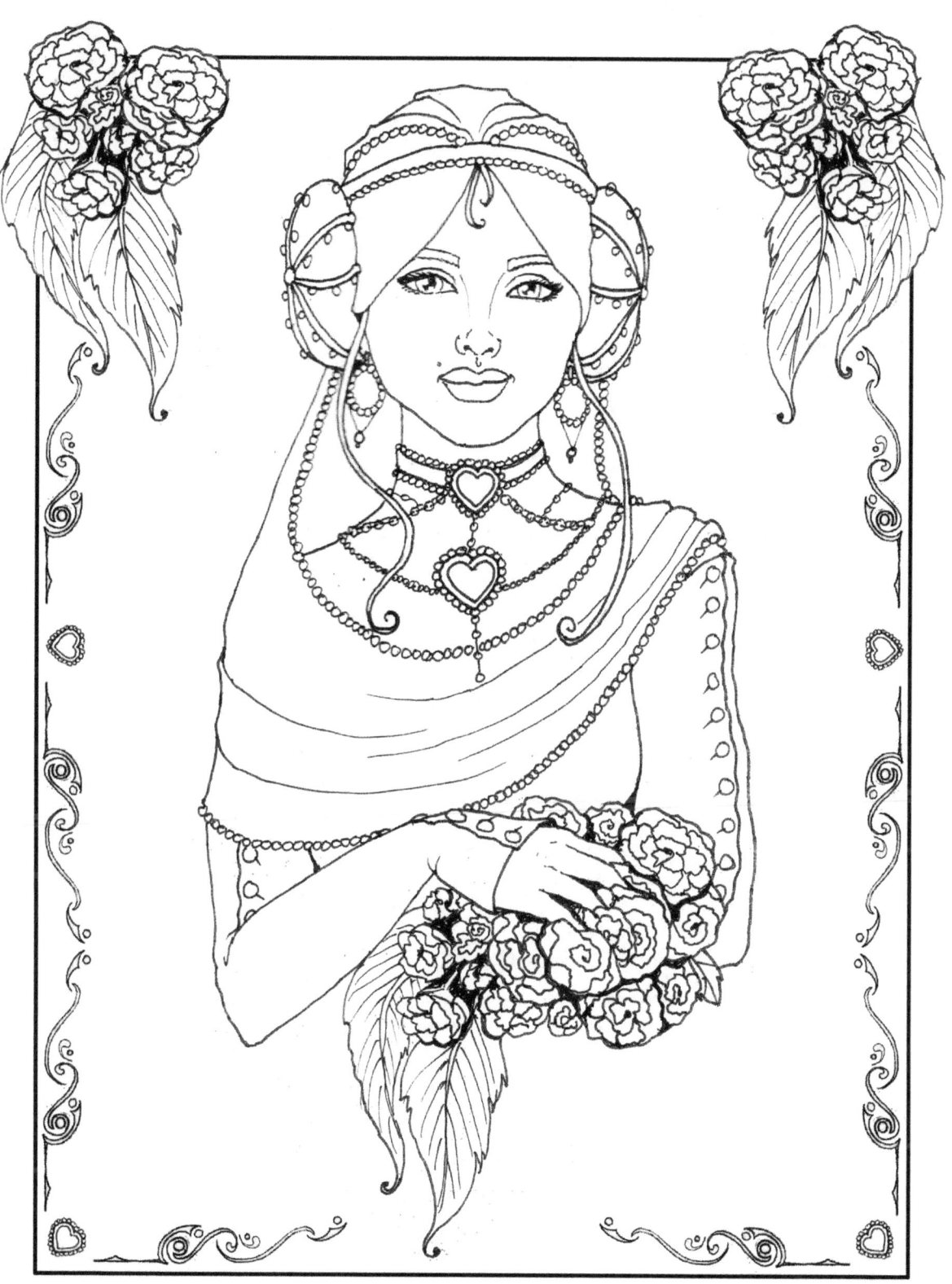

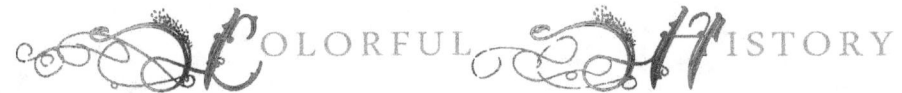
LEODOGRAN, THE KING OF CAMELIARD,

HAD ONE FAIR DAUGHTER, AND NONE OTHER CHILD;

AND SHE WAS FAIREST OF ALL FLESH ON EARTH,

GUINEVERE, AND IN HER HIS ONE DELIGHT.

(ALFRED, LORD TENNYSON)

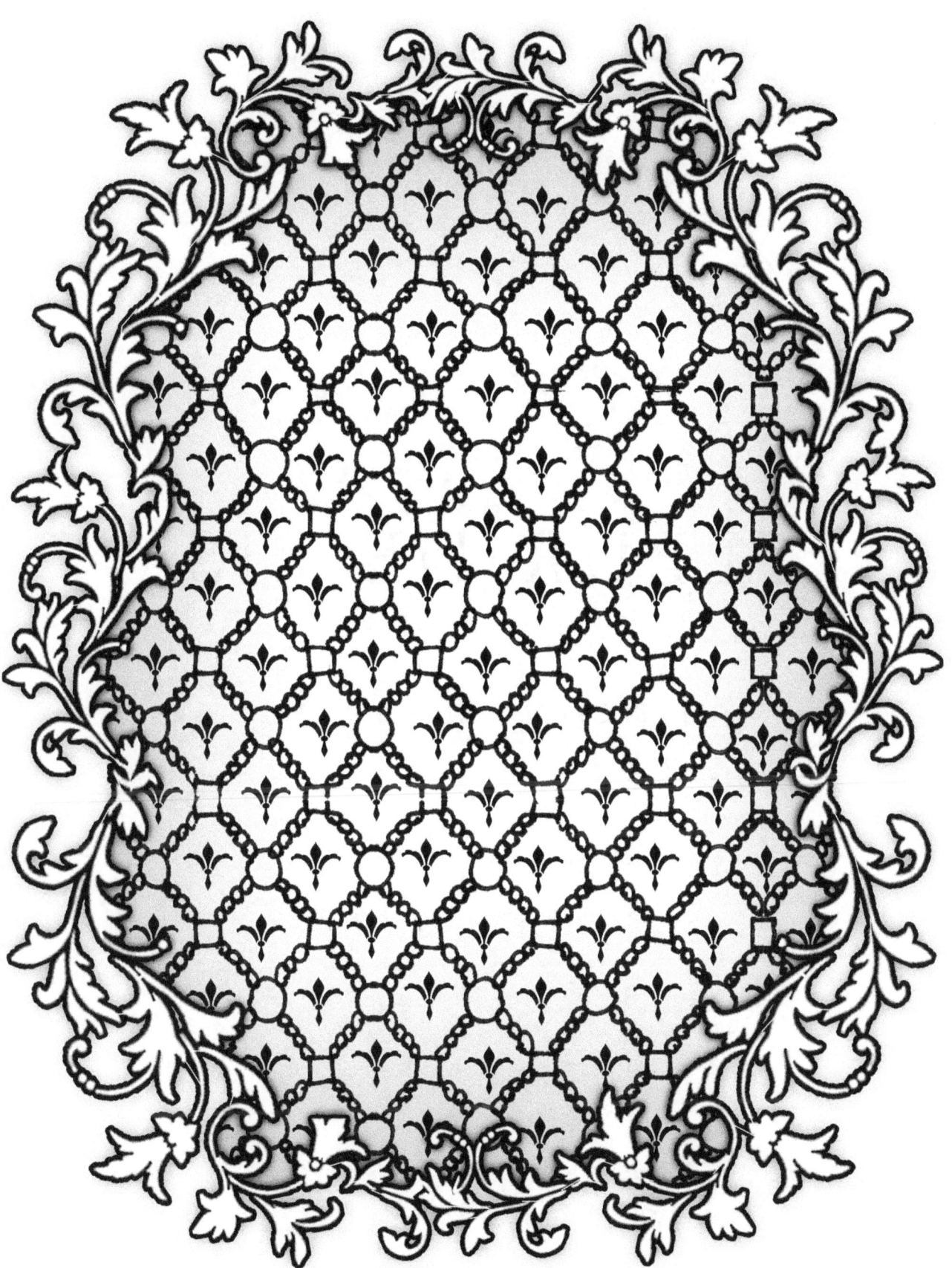

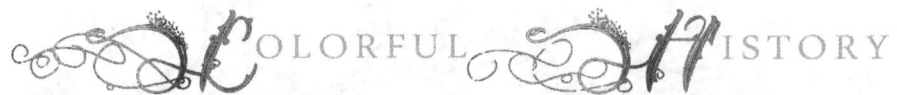
# THE FLEUR DE LIS

## PERFECTION . LIGHT . LIFE

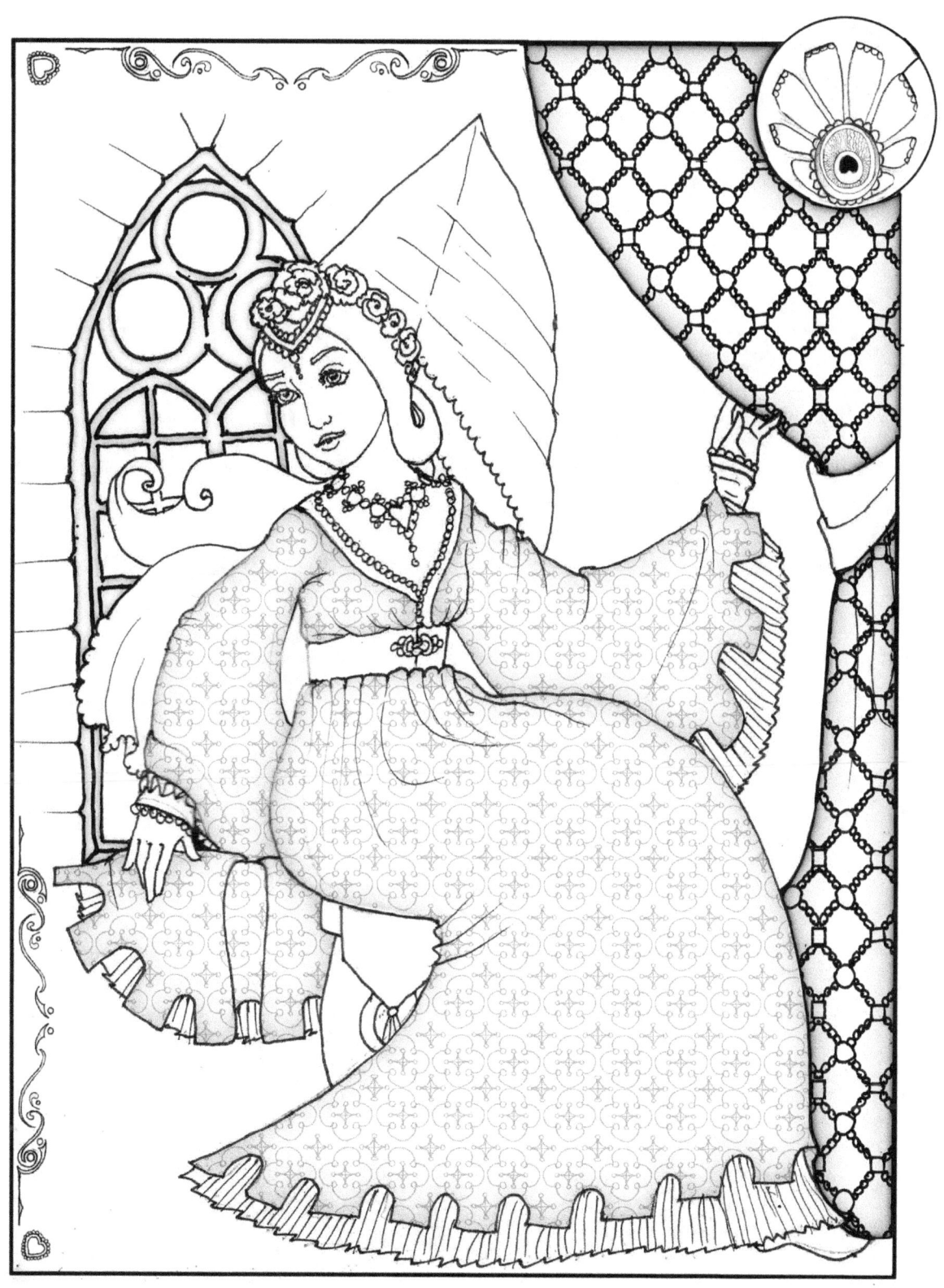

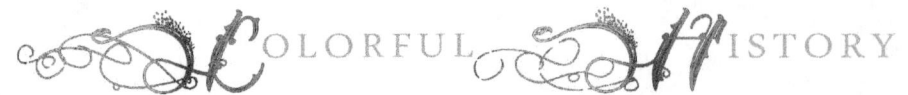

THE DOWNWARD GLANCE, THE RAISED BROW: MY BELOVED'S SMILE LIKE A MOONBEAM GLINTING

AS WE DANCED IN THE COURTYARD'S AUTUMN SUNSET AMONG OUR FRIENDS A'MINGLING

THE SOFT TOUCH OF MY LOVER'S HAND SET THE BARB DEEP WITHIN MY SOUL

I FOUND MY KNEES FOR HER, SWORE MY LIFE FOR HER, AS A VASSAL OFFERED WHOLE

BUT SHE BLUSHING TURNED HER HEAD, AND SO WINTER CAME UPON ME SINKING

BUT WHO AM I TO DARE MY LOVER'S VIRTUE, THOUGH DEEP BARB'S WOUND IS BLEEDING

THE BLOOD IT SHEDS IN RIVERS IS SWORN HERS BY RIGHT

AND I WILL BE CONTENT TO JUST LINGER NEAR HER LIGHT.


(SEAMUS KING)

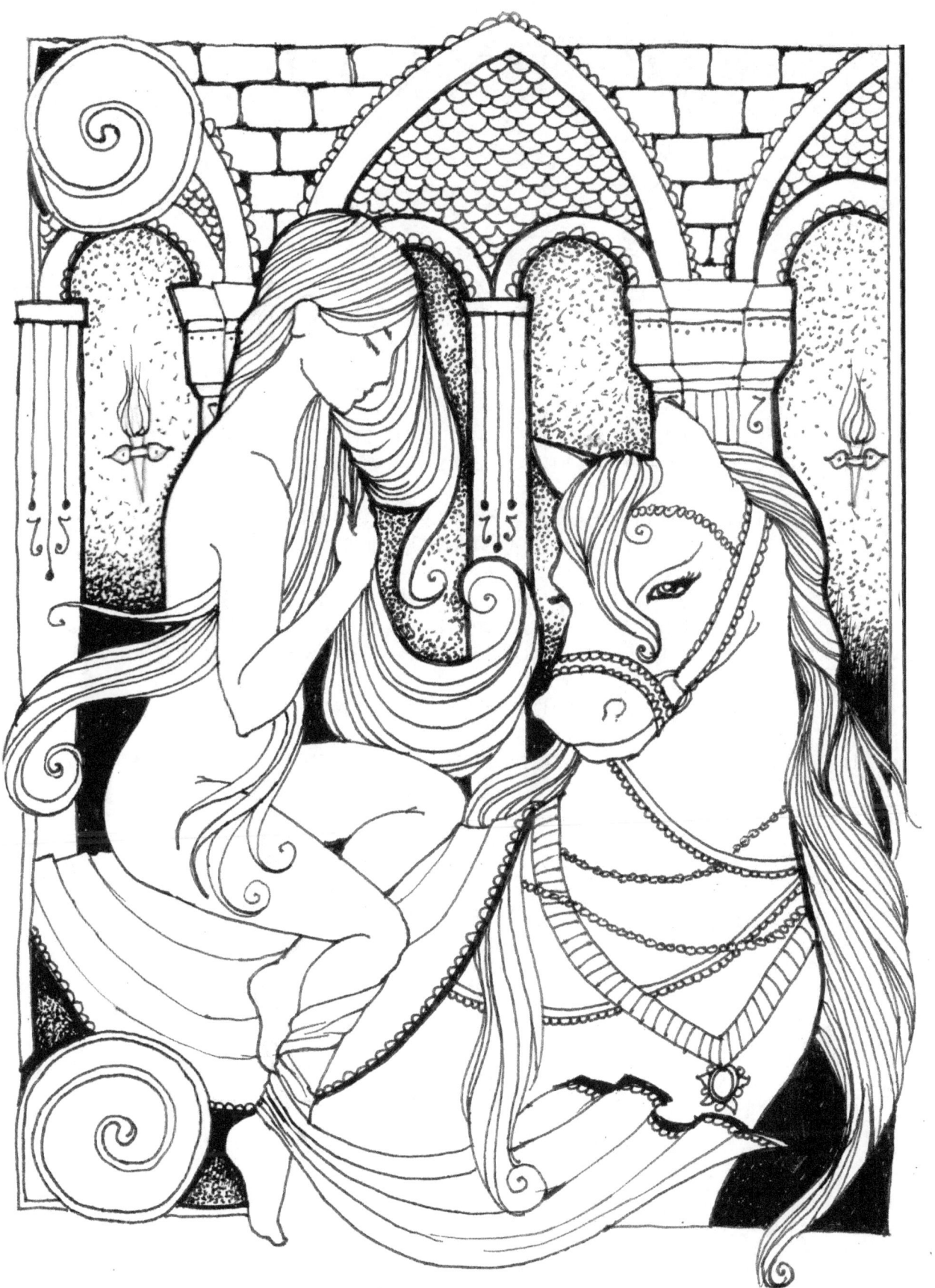

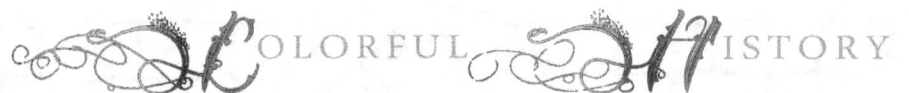

AND LO SHE RODE, THROUGH THE STREETS,
CLAD IN NAUGHT BUT THE GLORY OF HER OWN HAIR.

AND THE PEOPLE OF HER TOWN TURNED AWAY THEIR GAZE,
FORBIDDEN A GLANCE OR STARE;

AND UP THE HILL SHE RODE,
TO THE GATES OF HER PALACE ON THE MOTTE,
IN ORDER THAT HER HUSBAND WOULD RIGHT THE WRONGS HE'D WROUGHT.

GODIVA, BRAVE GODIVA, CLAD JUST IN HAIR AND SKY,

RODE BOLDLY FOR HER PEOPLE, AND RODE WITH HEAD HELD HIGH.


(SEAMUS KING)

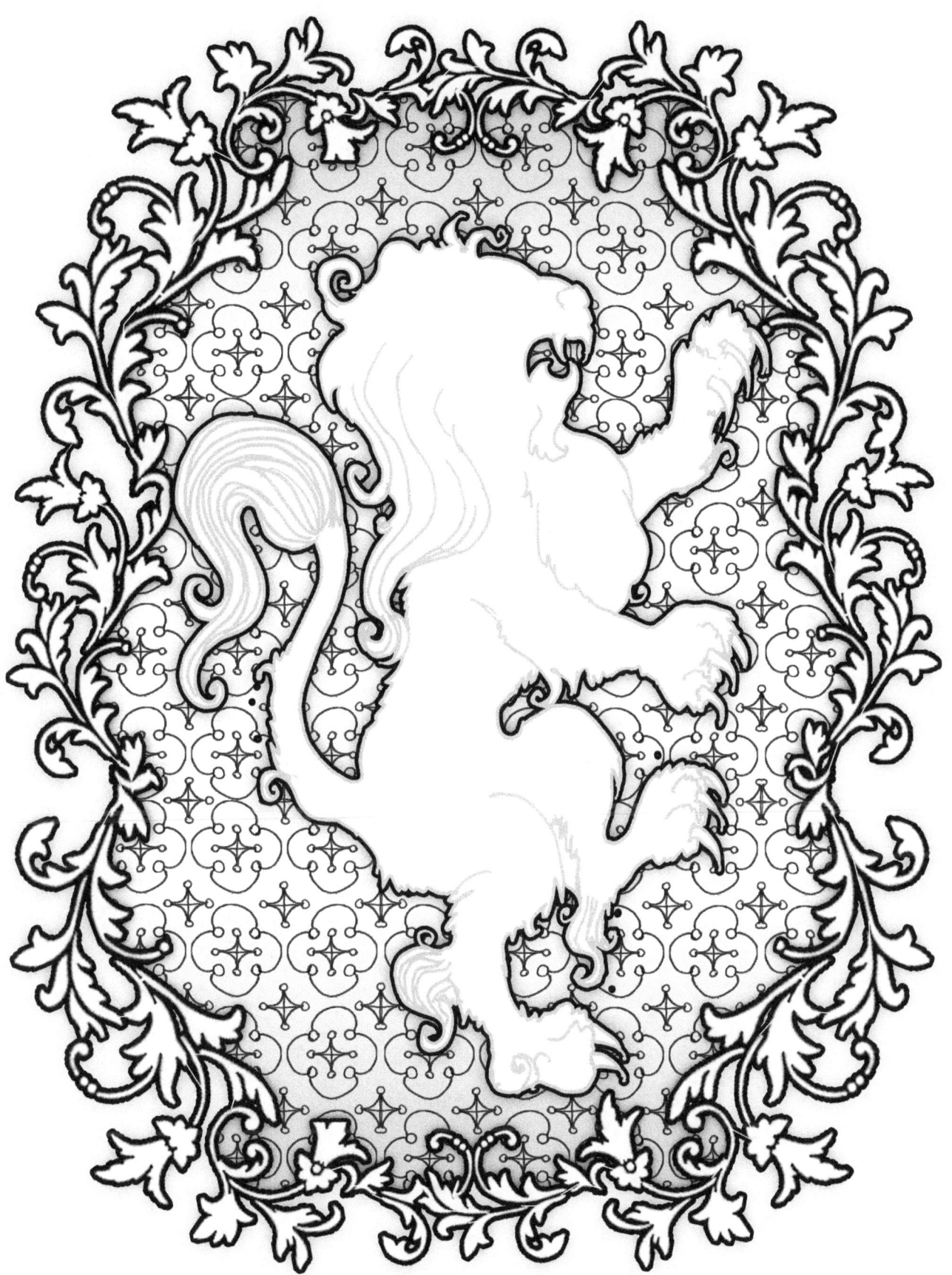

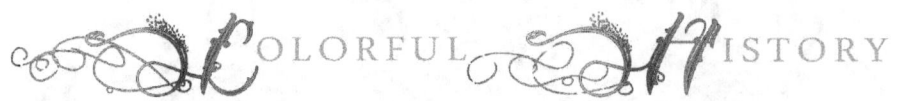
# THE
# LION

### STRENGTH . VALOUR . FEROCITY

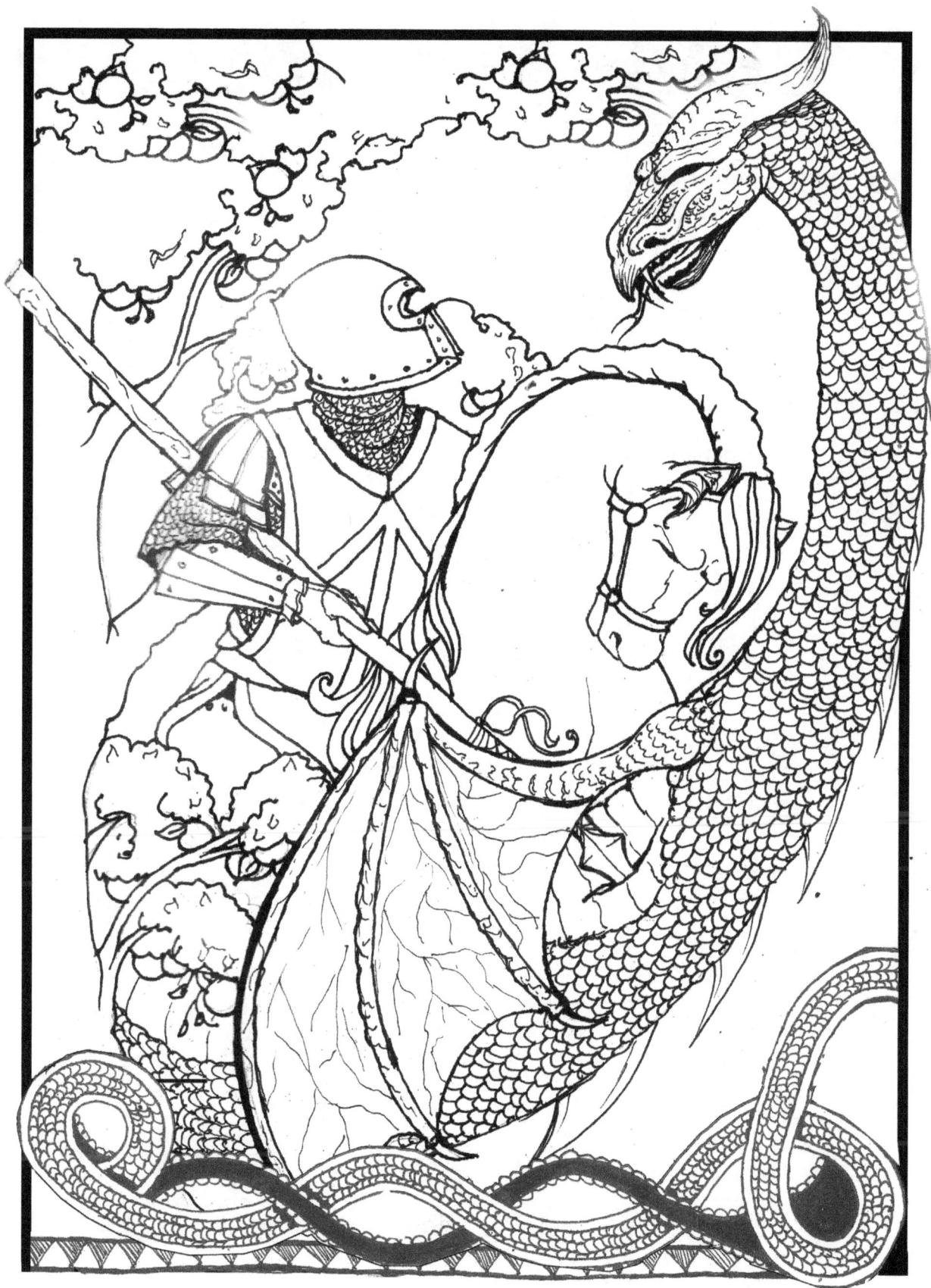

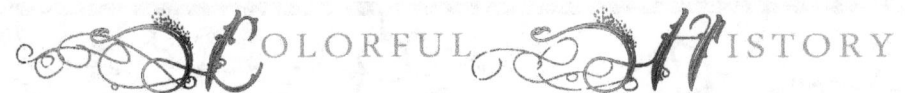

# COLORFUL HISTORY

AND GEORGE CAME A' RIDING, HIS ARMOR CHINKING, HIS SPEAR-HEAD GLEAMING,

TO FACE THE DRAGON IN ITS SCALES SLINKING.

THRICE HE RODE AGAINST NATURE'S BLIGHTING, LANCE A'STRIKING, HIS ASHEN SHAFT INTO DRAGON-SKIN BITING;

BUT THE DRAGON IN ITS FURY DID NOT STOP FIGHTING.

THE BOLD SAINT'S HORSE WAS SLAUGHTERED, HIS LANCE-SHAFT SHATTERED, HIS SHIELD SPLINTERED;

AND BY THE DRAGON'S BREATH, WHITE-FLAME HOT, HE WAS NEAR MURDERED.

BUT BY GOD'S GRACE HE STOOD UN-BURN'D, FOR THROUGH THE CROSS HE ENDUR'D, AND ALL AROUND IT COULD BE HEAR'D.

AS HIS BATTLE CRY HE HURL'D.

ONCE HIS SWORD DID RISE, AND AS A STAR IT FELL, ITS BLOW A RINGING BELL, A MESSAGE SENT TO HELL

AND ALL THOSE BELOW WHO IN IT DWELL.

AGAIN THE SWORD DID RISE, AND UNTO GOD HE CRIED, AND WITH A MIGHTY HEW HE DRIVED

HIS LAST BLOW HOME… AND THE DRAGON DIED.

(SEAMUS KING)

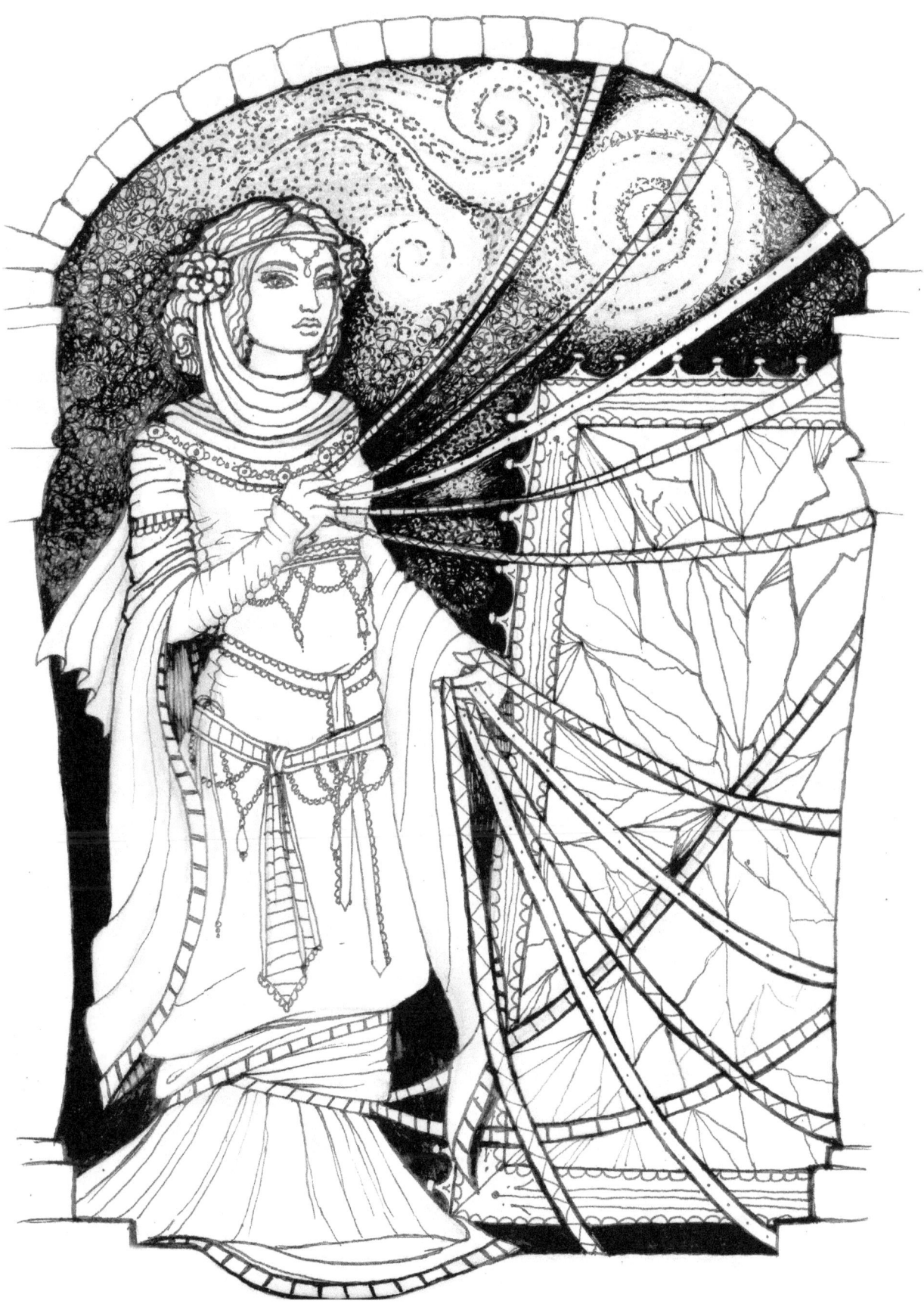

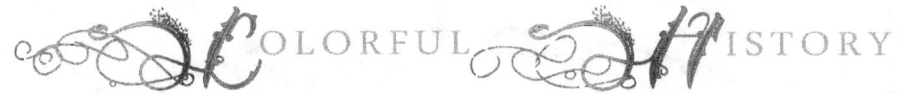

NO TIME HATH SHE TO SPORT AND PLAY:

A CHARMED WEB SHE WEAVES ALWAY.

A CURSE IS ON HER, IF SHE STAY

HER WEAVING, EITHER NIGHT OR DAY,

TO LOOK DOWN TO CAMELOT.

SHE KNOWS NOT WHAT THE CURSE MAY BE;

THEREFORE SHE WEAVETH STEADILY,

THEREFORE NO OTHER CARE HATH SHE,

THE LADY OF SHALOTT.


(ALFRED, LORD TENNYSON)

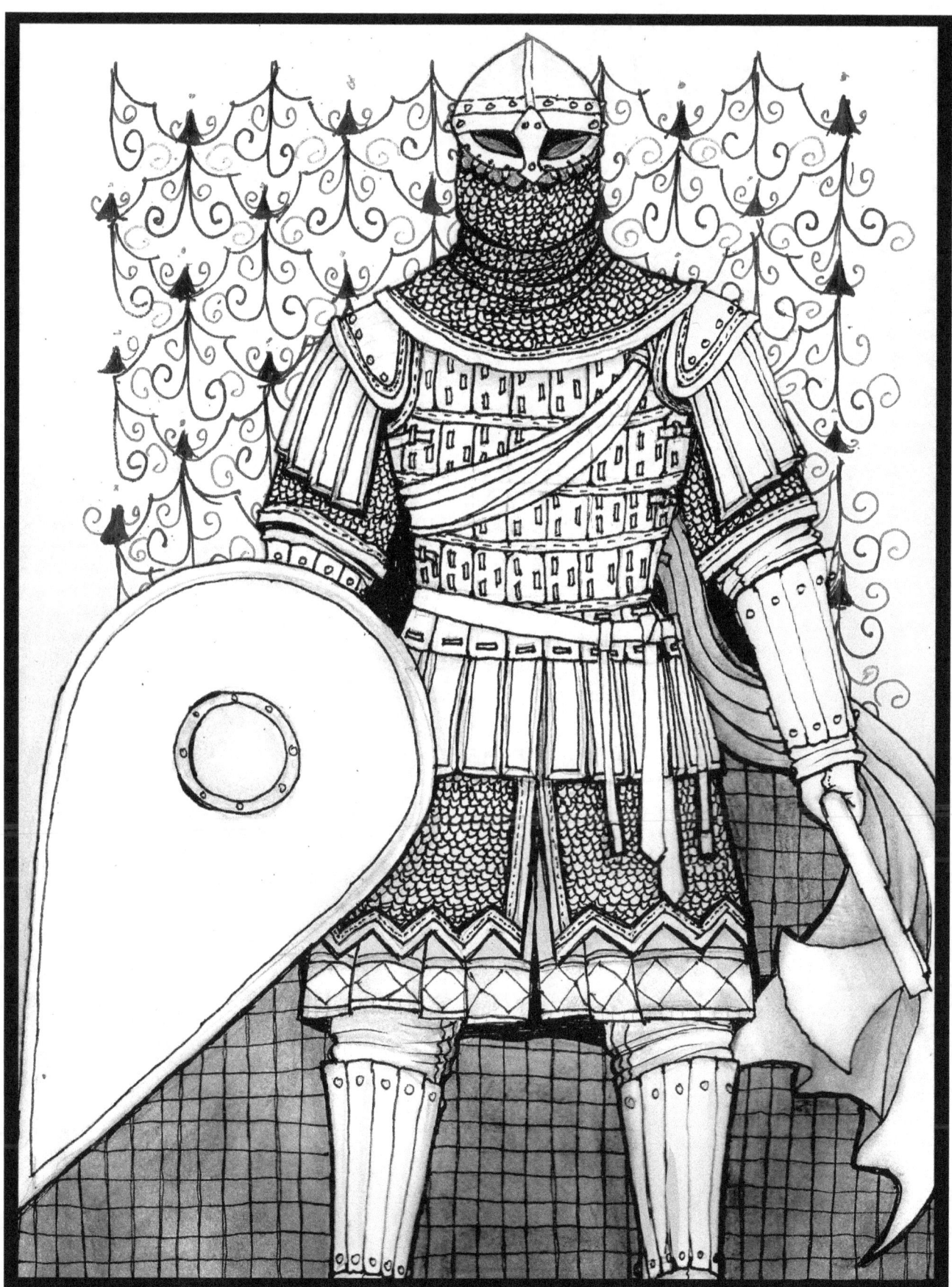

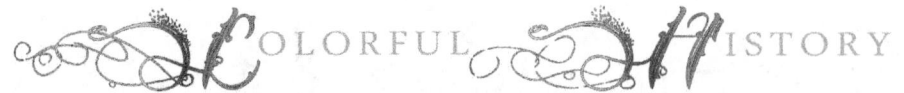

## THE VARANGIAN

…AND THE MEN FROM THE NORTH, WARRIORS THAT SERVED

VLADIMIR OF KIEV, WERE SENT DOWN TO CONSTANTINOPLE

(WHICH THEY CALLED MIKLAGARD) TO FUFILL THE TREATY.

SIX THOUSAND MEN, LONG OF LIMB AND STRONG OF SINEW,

STOOD TO STAND BESIDE THEIR EMPEROR.  WITH THEIR HEAVY

SHIELDS AND THEIR SINGLE-EDGED AXES THEY WOULD GUARD

THE GREAT JARL OF THE BYZANTINES WITH THEIR LIFE,

AND SUCH WAS THEIR SAVAGERY THAT THEY WOULD

CUT DOWN THE ENEMY EVEN AS THEY FLED.


(SEAMUS KING)

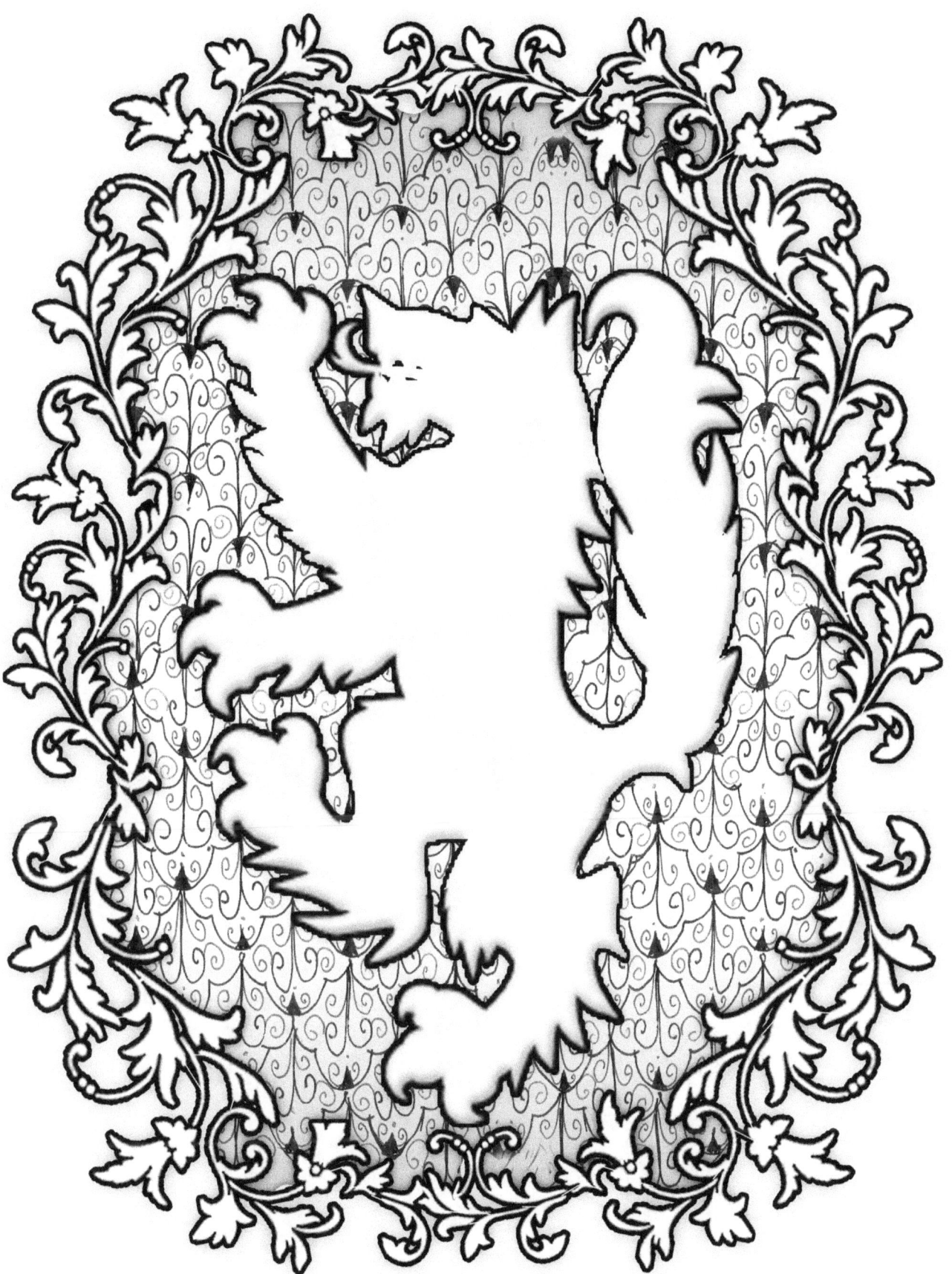

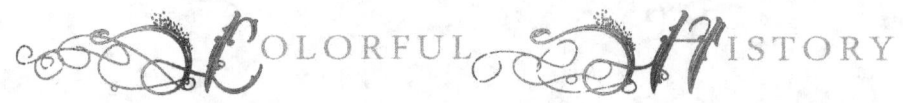

THE
# WOLF

VICTORY THROUGH ENDURANCE

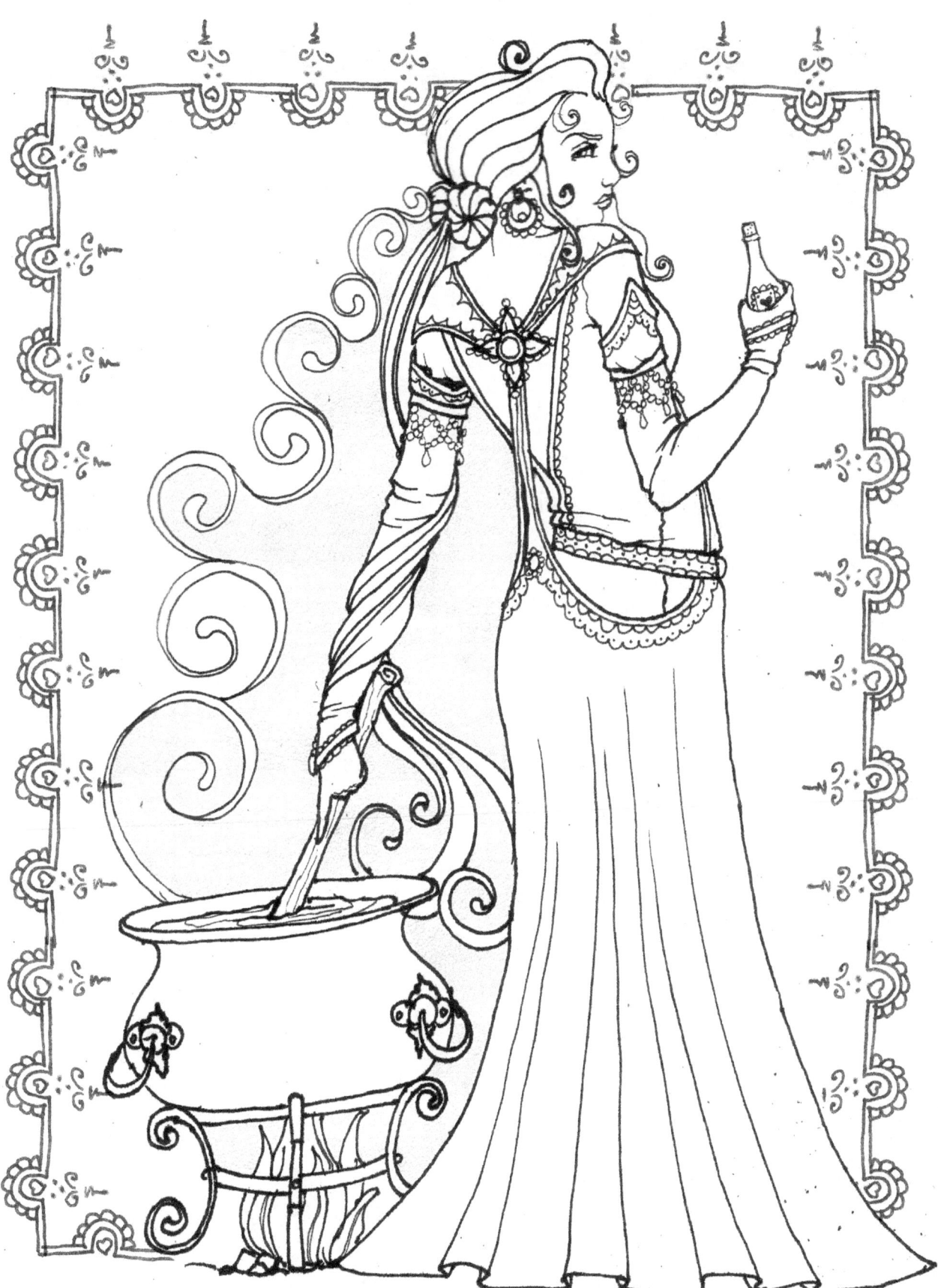

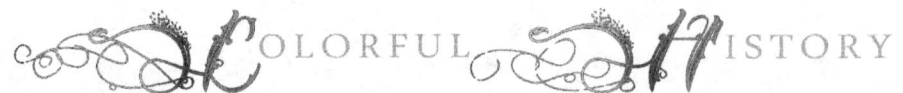

O, THEN, I SEE QUEEN MAB HATH BEEN WITH YOU.

SHE IS THE FAIRIES' MIDWIFE, AND SHE COMES

IN SHAPE NO BIGGER THAN AN AGATE-STONE

ON THE FORE-FINGER OF AN ALDERMAN,

DRAWN WITH A TEAM OF LITTLE ATOMIES

ATHWART MEN'S NOSES AS THEY LIE ASLEEP


(SHAKESPEARE, ROMEO AND JULIET)

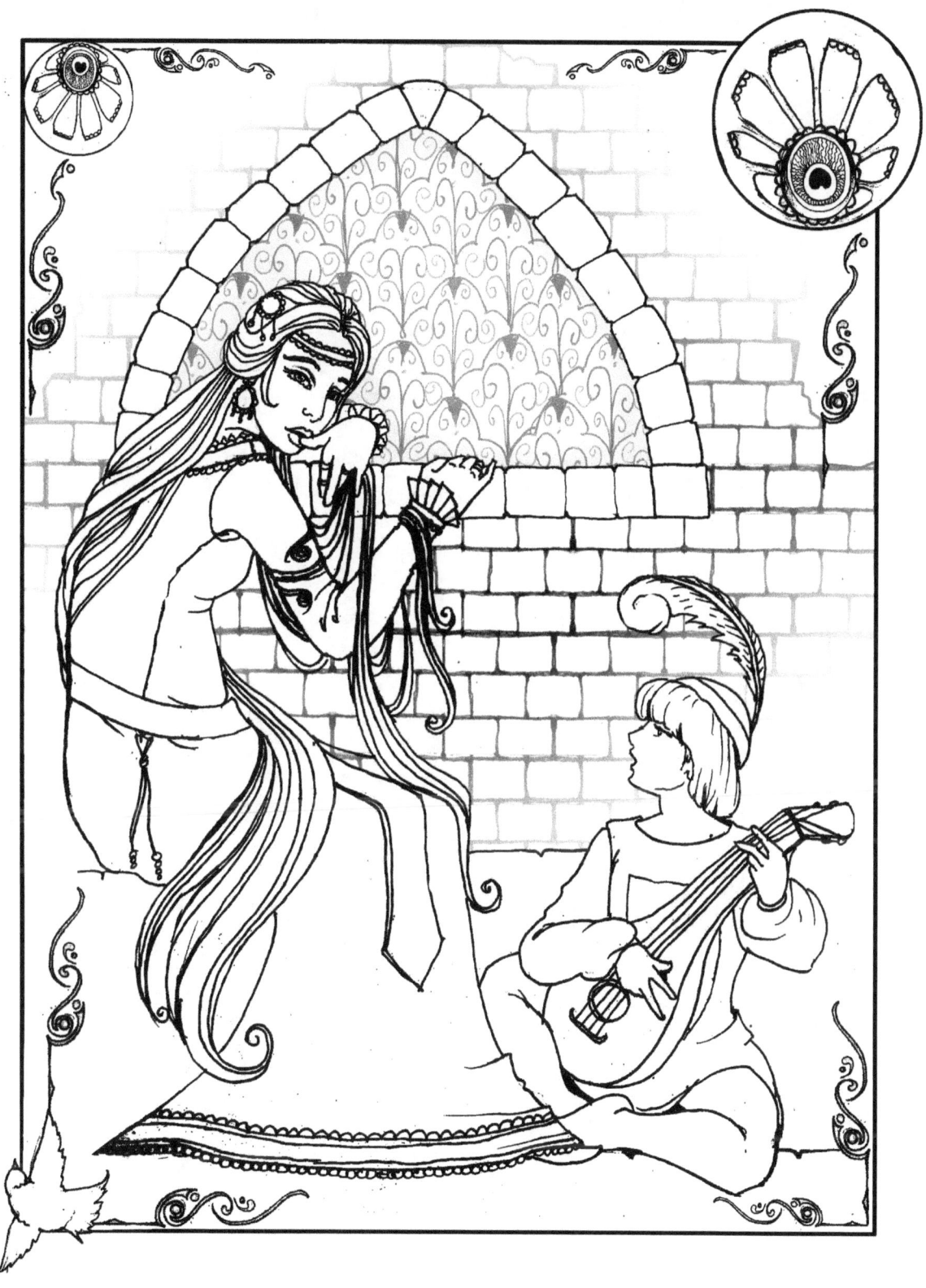

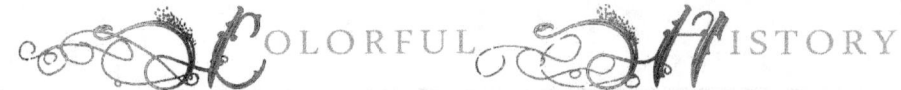

Eleanor of Aquitaine (1122-1204) was Queen-consort of both France (1137-1152) and England (1154-1189). She was the mother of three Kings, Henry (reigning at the same time as his father until his death), Richard, and John, and two queens- Eleanor and Joan. But her power was not due purely to her husbands, august though they were. She was a fierce and powerful woman all on her own. Duchess of Aquitaine in her own right by the time she was fifteen, she went to Crusade with her first husband, King Louis VII and raised a revolt against King Henry. She hosted courts in Potiers that helped encourage and catalyze the romantic poems and troubadour artistry that was just taking off in the twelfth century, combining the concepts of an idealized form of chivalry with the idea of courtly love and an appreciation for beauty that so define the stereotypical image of the high medieval period.

By all accounts, in both wealth and influence she was one of the most powerful women of her time, perhaps of all time, and her story has fascinated historians for generations. She has been portrayed in many movies, the most notable perhaps being The Lion in Winter, a stage play that made it into movie form twice. Eleanor was portrayed by Katherine Hepburn in the first rendition, Glen Close in the second, and in both examples the movie really revolves around her cunning and savvy at interpersonal politics. In truth, she has never really left the imaginations of historians: she is the prototypical Queen, powerful, cunning, and driven to excel beyond the limitations placed on her sex.

For further reading, I suggest the April Queen by Douglas Boyd. It provides an excellent insight to Eleanor's life and times, examining her cultural background, the scope of her marriages, and the controversies the queen often found herself embroiled in.

(SEAMUSTHEKING.COM)

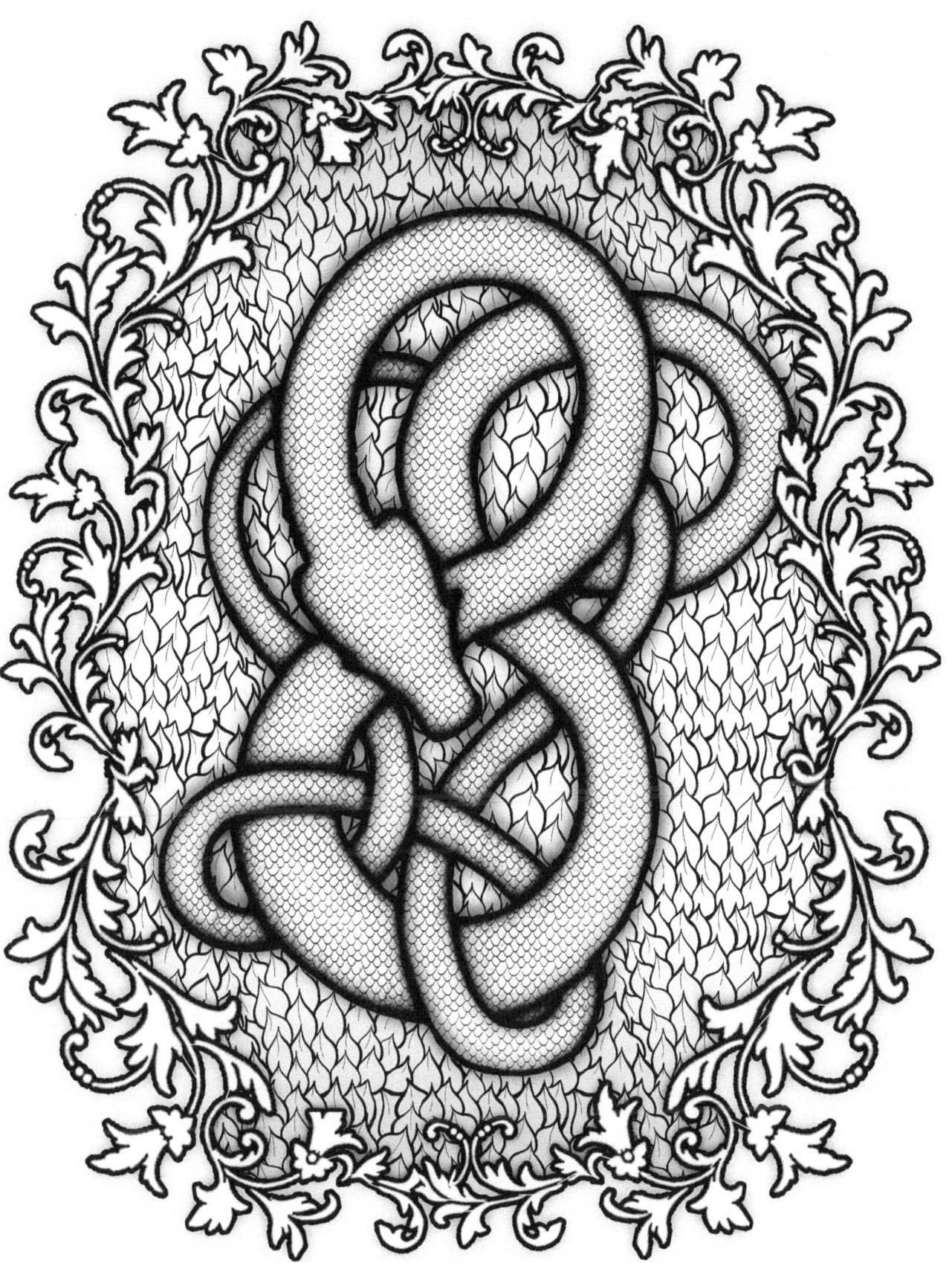

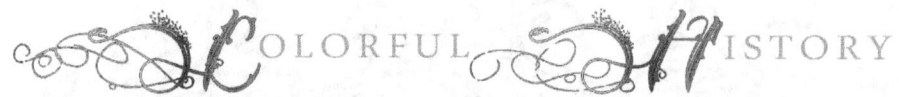

# THE
# SERPENT

WISDOM . CREATIVITY . RENEWAL

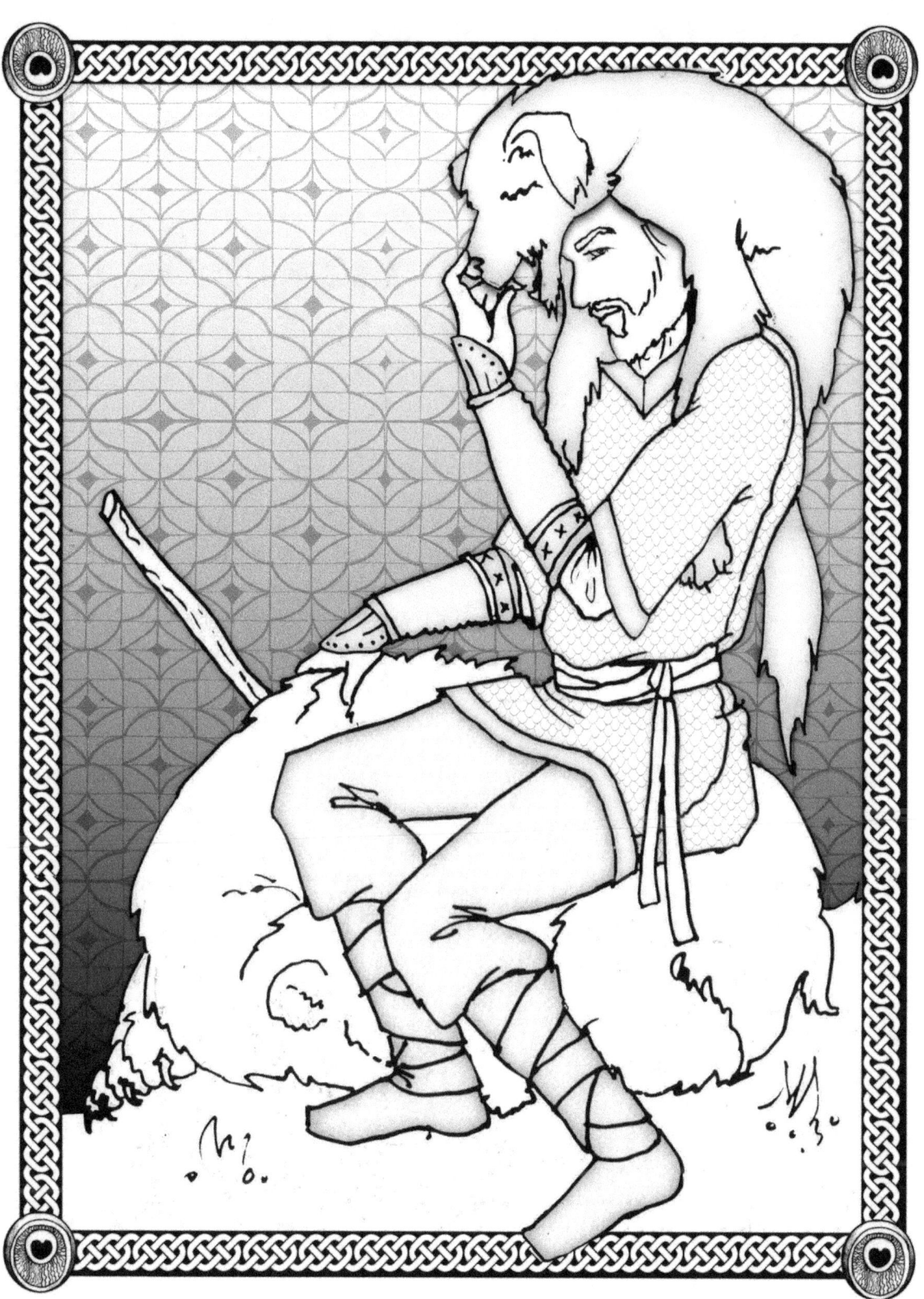

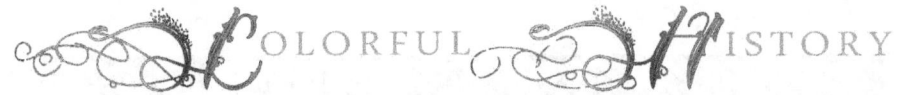

"AND SO RAGNAR'S EYES FELL ON BOLD LAGERTHA
FIERCE LIKE THE THUNDERER'S LAUGHTER,
FAIR AS FROST ON STEEL
AND SWORE BY THE AMBER-TEARED HE'D MAKE HER HIS
BUT THE WILD-EYED MAIDEN WOULD HAVE NO MAN
THAT COULD NOT BEST BOTH BEAR AND HOUND
AND SO THE YEARNING-HEART MET BOTH BEASTS…. "


(SEAMUS KING)

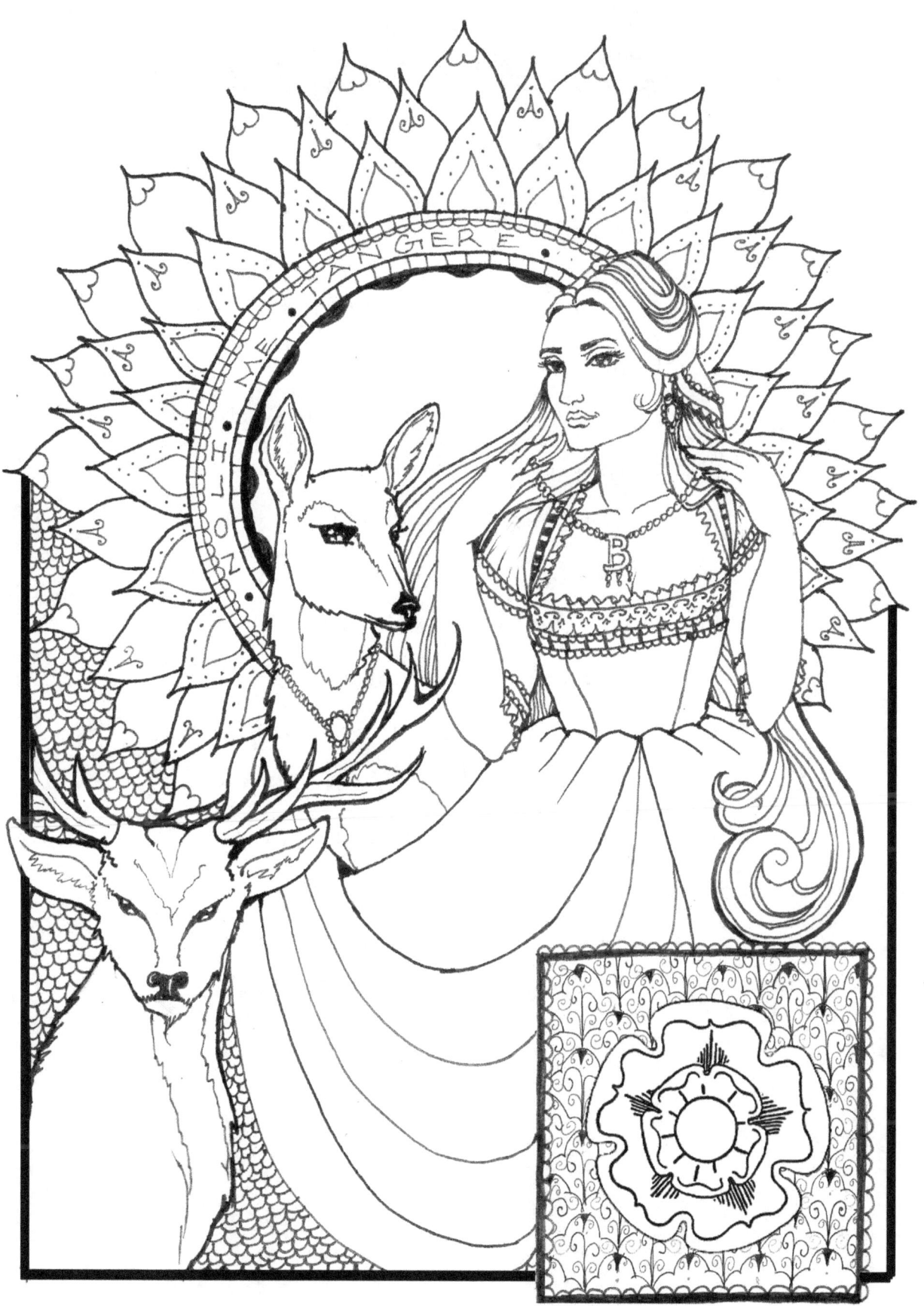

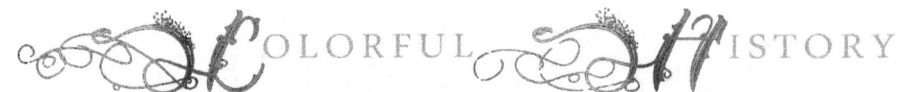

WHOSO LIST TO HUNT, I KNOW WHERE IS AN HIND,

BUT AS FOR ME, HÉLAS, I MAY NO MORE.

THE VAIN TRAVAIL HATH WEARIED ME SO SORE,

I AM OF THEM THAT FARTHEST COMETH BEHIND.

YET MAY I BY NO MEANS MY WEARIED MIND

DRAW FROM THE DEER, BUT AS SHE FLEETH AFORE

FAINTING I FOLLOW. I LEAVE OFF THEREFORE,

SITHENS IN A NET I SEEK TO HOLD THE WIND.

WHO LIST HER HUNT, I PUT HIM OUT OF DOUBT,

AS WELL AS I MAY SPEND HIS TIME IN VAIN.

AND GRAVEN WITH DIAMONDS IN LETTERS PLAIN

THERE IS WRITTEN, HER FAIR NECK ROUND ABOUT:

NOLI ME TANGERE, FOR CAESAR'S I AM,

AND WILD FOR TO HOLD, THOUGH I SEEM TAME.

(SIR THOMAS WYATT)

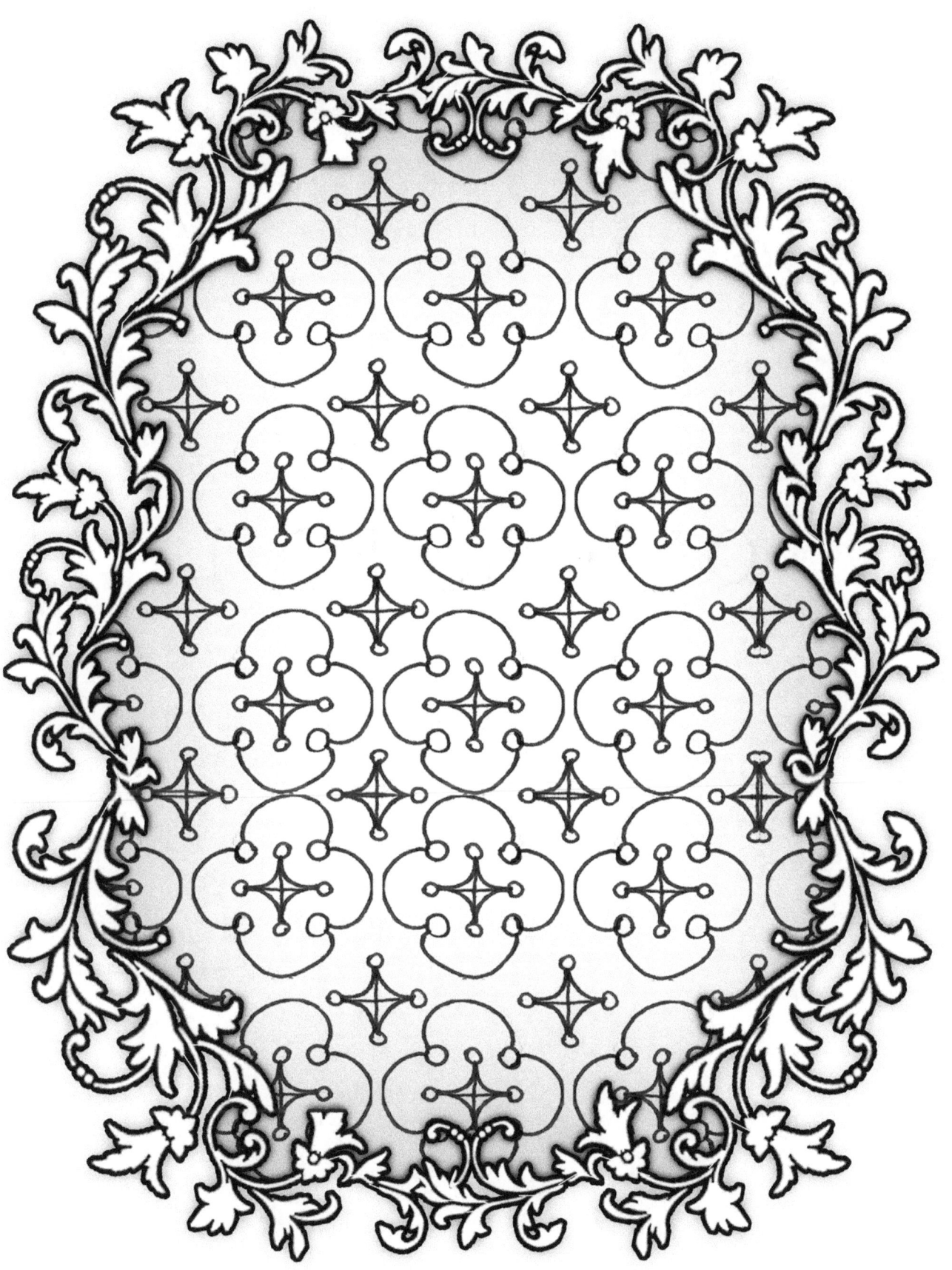

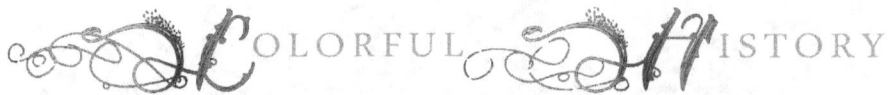
# THE
# QUATREFOIL

"FOUR LEAVES", FROM LATIN QUATTUOR, FOUR, PLUS FOLIUM, A LEAF.

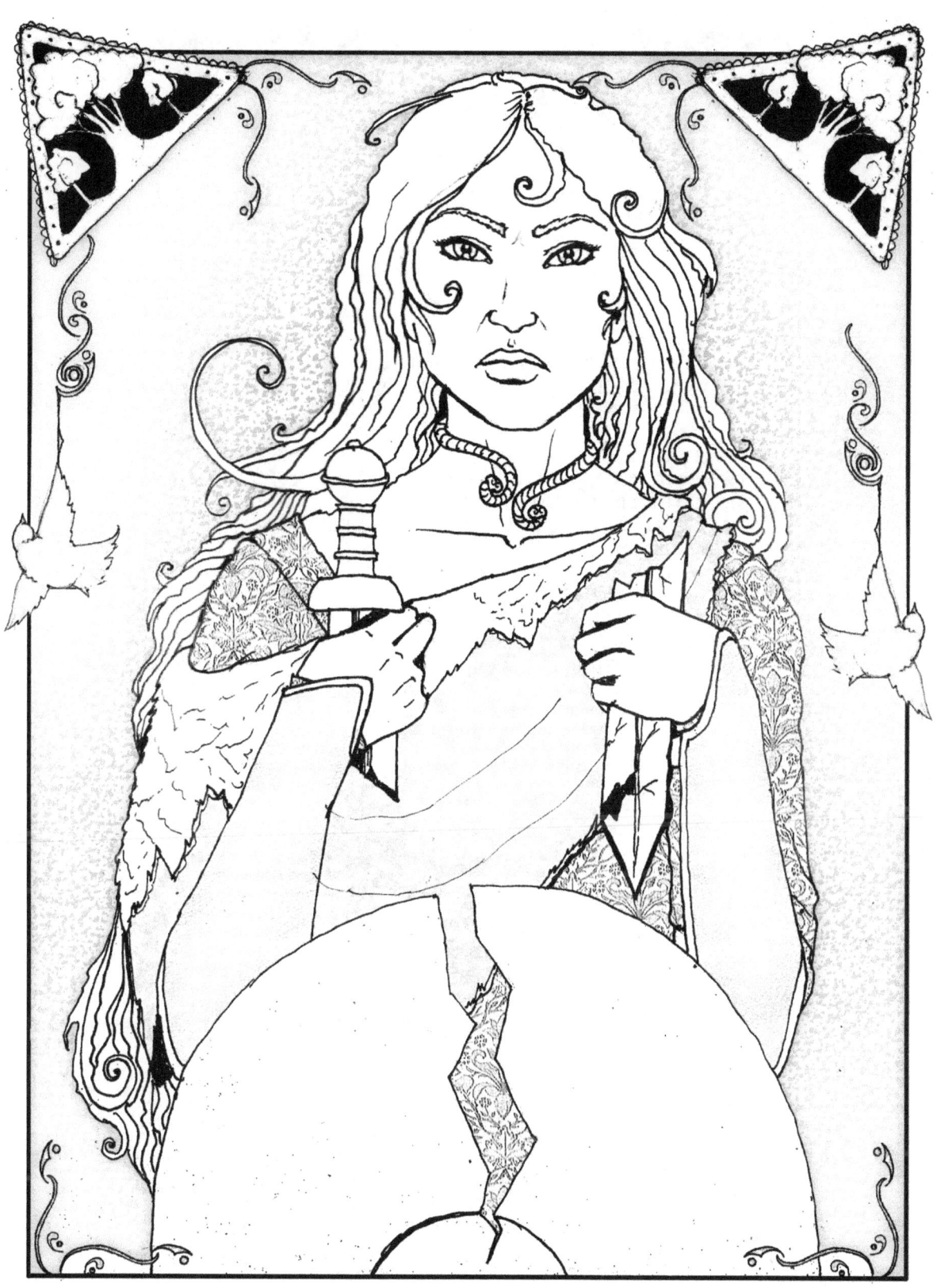

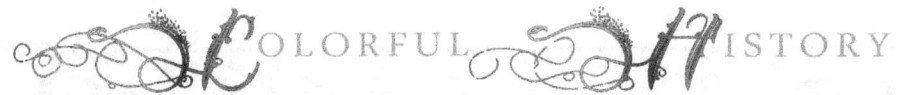
"WE WILL NOT BOW TO THESE INVADERS FROM THE SOUTH.
WE WILL NOT BEND OUR KNEE, WE WILL GIVE THEM NEITHER SILVER NOR SUCCOR.
WE WILL GIVE NONE OF OUR YOUNG MEN TO FIGHT THEIR WARS NOR OUR DAUGHTERS
TO SLATE THEIR LUSTS.
WE WILL GIVE THEM THEIR DUE.
WE WILL GIVE THEM THE POINTS OF OUR SPEARS;
WE WILL GIVE THEM THE EDGE OF OUR AXES.
WE WILL GIVE THEM FIRE, AND WE WILL GIVE THEM TERROR,
AND WE WILL GIVE THEM DEATH.
TOGETHER WE ARE STRONG! RISE! RISE WITH ME NOW,
AND RECLAIM OUR LANDS FROM ROME!"

THE ICENI, A BRITTONIC TRIBE IN EASTERN BRITAIN IN THE IRON AGE, INITIALLY
TRADED WITH AND ALLIED WITH THE ROMANS DURING CLAUDIUS'S INVASION (AD 43).
BUT THE NATURE OF ROME IS TO MEDDLE, AND BY THE TIME OF THE KING
PRASUTAGUS'S DEATH IN AD 60 THEY SOUGHT TO CLAIM HIS LANDS ENTIRELY.
WHEN HIS WIFE, NOMINAL HEIR, RESISTED, SHE WAS BEATEN AND HER DAUGHTERS
ABUSED.

THIS WOULD NOT STAND.
HER NAME NOW FOREVER WRITTEN INTO THE FABRIC OF HISTORY, BOUDICA ROSE
AGAINST THE ROMANS WITH ALL THE FURY OF HER PEOPLE. THE REVOLT WAS HUGE,
AND MANAGED TO BURN THREE CITIES, INCLUDING LONDINIUM, BEFORE THEY WERE
FINALLY DEFEATED BY THE ROMANS. A STATUE OF BOUDICA, WIELDING A SWORD
UPON A CHARIOT, STILL STANDS TO THIS DAY, AN IMMORTAL REMINDER OF THE
FIERCENESS OF HER PEOPLE.

(SEAMUS KING)

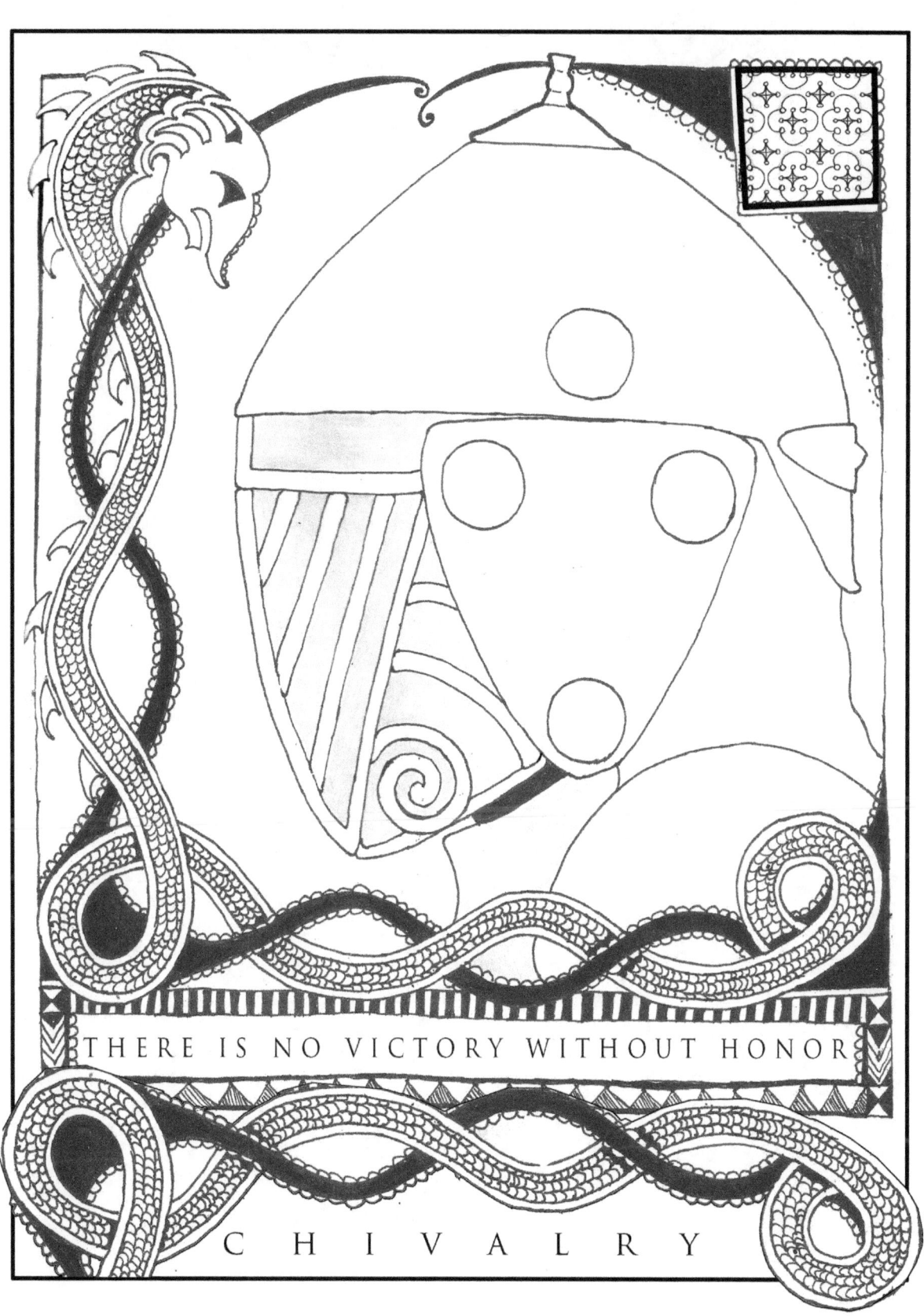

THERE IS NO VICTORY WITHOUT HONOR

C H I V A L R Y

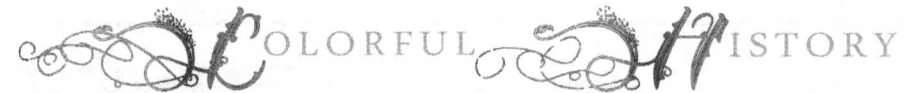

THE IDEA OF CHIVALRY, A TERM ONCE REFERRING SOLELY TO ONE'S

SKILL WITH A HORSE, TOOK ON NEW LIFE WITHIN THE IMAGINATIONS

AND STORIES OF TWELFTH-CENTURY TROUBADOURS.

IT BEGAN TO REPRESENT AN IDEAL OF BEHAVIOR,

A COMBINATION OF BOTH PROWESS AND GENTILITY.

(SEAMUS KING)

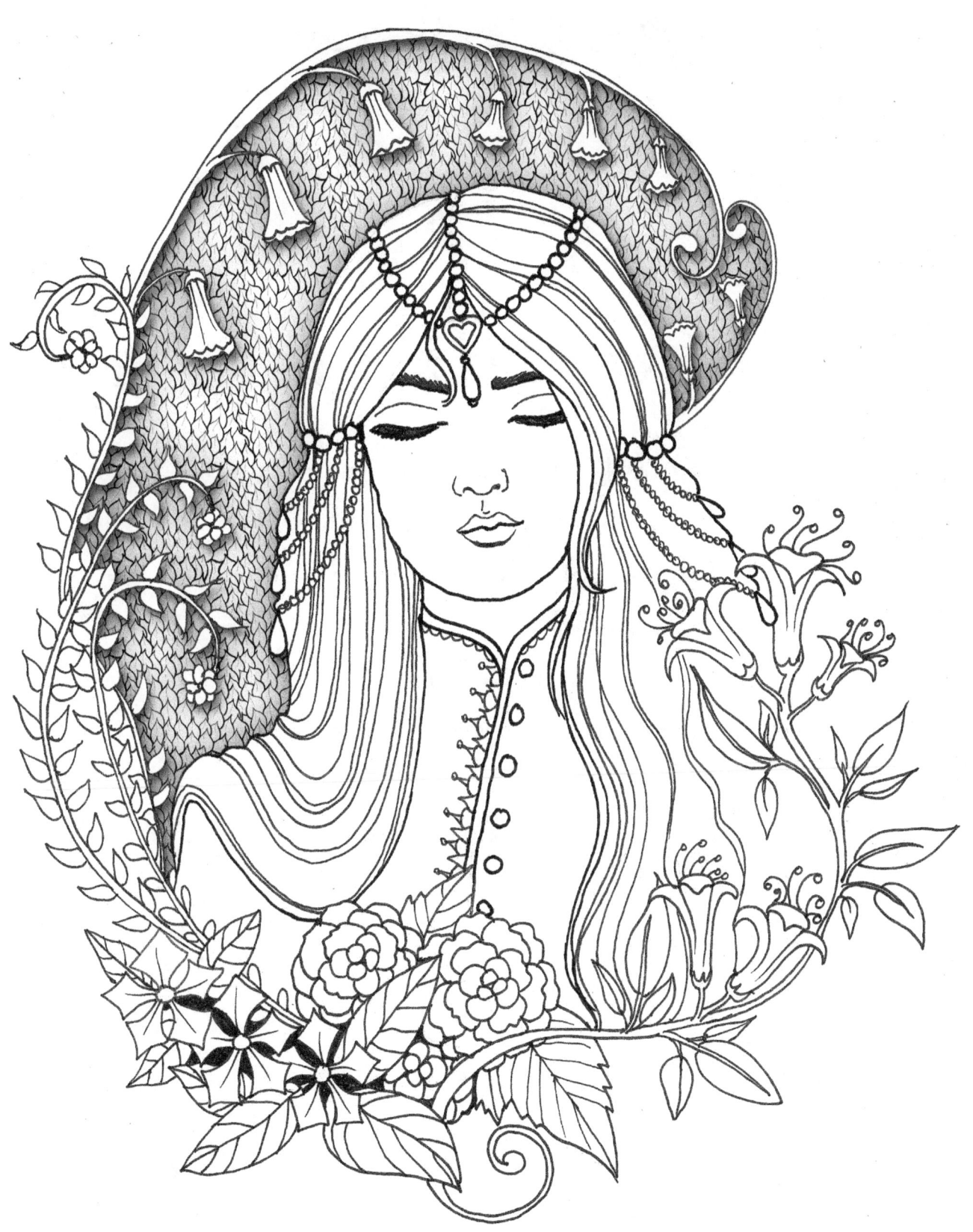

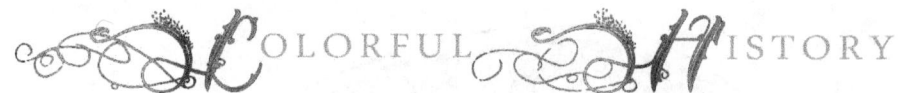

I KNOW A BANK WHERE THE WILD THYME BLOWS,

WHERE OXLIPS AND THE NODDING VIOLET GROWS,

QUITE OVER-CANOPIED WITH LUSCIOUS WOODBINE,

WITH SWEET MUSK-ROSES AND WITH EGLANTINE:

THERE SLEEPS TITANIA SOMETIME OF THE NIGHT,

LULL'D IN THESE FLOWERS WITH DANCES AND DELIGHT

(SHAKESPEARE, A MIDSUMMER NIGHT'S DREAM)